All There Is To Lose

All There Is To Lose

Aiden Heung

Four Way Books
Tribeca

For my parents and grandparents

For people who have lived—or still live—in the tiny village called 915, in the heart of Muli Tibetan Autonomous County, Sichuan, China

The past is a foreign country: they do things differently there.

Library of Congress Cataloging-in-Publication Data

Names: Heung, Aiden author
Title: All there is to lose / Aiden Heung.
Description: New York : Four Way Books, 2026.
Identifiers: LCCN 2025027260 (print) | LCCN 2025027261 (ebook) | ISBN 9781961897687 trade paperback | ISBN 9781961897694 ebook
Subjects: LCGFT: Poetry
Classification: LCC PS3608.E896 A78 2026 (print) | LCC PS3608.E896 (ebook) | DDC 811/.6--dc23/eng/20250623
LC record available at https://lccn.loc.gov/2025027260
LC ebook record available at https://lccn.loc.gov/2025027261

This book is manufactured in the United States of America and printed on acid-free paper.

Funding for this book was provided in part by a generous donation in memory of John J. Wilson.

Four Way Books is a not-for-profit literary press. We are grateful for the assistance we receive from individual donors, public arts agencies, and private foundations including the New York State Council on the Arts, a state agency.

We are a proud member of the Community of Literary Magazines and Presses.

Contents

At the End of the World 3

I

Elegy 7
On the Slope of the Dead 8
The Shrine 9
Mother Gifted Me to the Mountain God 10
What Remained 11
Chess 13
Crossing 14
Oracle 15
Leaving 16

II

Elegy 21
When the Heavenly Dog Swallowed the Sun 22
Full Moon Ghazal 23
Pioneer 25
Inheritance 27
The Visit 28
The Man from the Mountain 29
Falling into Earth 30
What Was Carried in the Dark 32

III

Elegy 35
Death Brought Many Images 36
Darkest Hour 37
Before He Hanged Himself 39
I Was Told About the Loop Around His Neck 40

Color of the Moon 42
In the Dark 43
Drowning of a Shepherdess 45
What the Dead Wanted 46
Tomb Sweeping 47

IV

Elegy 51
Once Upon a Time 52
Looking for Shambhala 54
Aubade 55
Snow Country 57
The Pavilion of Flying Clouds 58
Drought 59
Ode 61
Gold 63
Chasing the Sun 65
In the Dream I Survived 68

V

Elegy 73
I Wake to a World That Has Rejected Me Many Times 74
Another Summer, Fujiang 76
Landscape for the Lost 78
Homebound 79
Muli 81
Like an Enemy, Like Love 83
End of the World 84
In the Hospital Mother Apologizes 88
Epilogue 90

Notes

At the End of the World

I carve their faces into stones and bury them. The valley is covered in ice. I sit where the land swallows sky: a golden eagle circles above, unsure whether to offer condolences; its wings scissor the crisp blue. The sun is colder than a touch. On my skin, the scent of rosin.

The village—a small handful of trellised dust—hides in imbricate ridges. A Tibetan woman knows the way. Her beaded braids sway snow as she turns away. I hear footfalls like bells. I reach out my hand; air flees from my grasp. If only I could be lifted like a thought. I offer myself, a mantra to a past undone piece by piece, atomized even. A surgeon of memory, I cut myself open.

I

Elegy

She loves the mountain. In her last sleep, she dreamed of soaring above the lasting green. *Sleep,* I said, pressing her hand as her hand pressed into my skin. If she must die, let her die like an echo.

An echo is never lost.

Ask the wind that passes it on. The wind, like a passing thought, brought back a note. She died. She was dead. I wrote in my book: *I'll bring her back—*

Moonlight shored against a pale moon. The land arched, reaching for the mountain she loved.

On the Slope of the Dead

Mother scrubs clean the headstone carvings,
layers of moss like kelp on a dry coast.
We've come a long way to this hirsute slope,
bypassing rocks, the brooding sentinels.
Our village, roofs wind-scoured, ducks
behind a corral of green. The sun
burns small as she arranges the offerings
in front of the stone—his name barely visible.
If forgetting could be this quick, this easy.

She calls out to him, expecting an answer:
perhaps a change of light, a stir in the woods,
a tremble of hands. I watch smoke rise
and fall into streaks of ash, leaving a sign
I don't understand. Mother knows. She kowtows
three times, mumbling words that soon wither.
Something lingers: a breath, a whisper.
I ask her what she said; she smiles, never so happy,
her eyes lifted to the billowing clouds.

The Shrine

The cable wire slashed off Mother's
finger. She fell—a doll
tossed down the cliff, broken.
For days the village elders tried
to chant life back into her body—her soul
was taken to a place they would not tell.
She remembered waking
to songs and gongs, and weeping as she gazed
at the stump of the finger—
a token reprieve from a dreadful fate.
Upon recovery, she built a shrine,
prayed at every sunrise;
her palms folded: a misshapen lotus.
I pried them open, counted
the calloused lines one by one
until I was lost in the intricate web.
Disheartened, I sentenced her,
with the cruelty of children,
to a miserable life. She knitted her brows,
pressed me into her arms—
every thump of her heart a drum
from a distant place.
Behind us, the mountain writhed,
a ruthless green.

Mother Gifted Me to the Mountain God

I was not yet seven. I liked her morning incense and evening songs. "Good to be a godling" she smiled, washing my head with sandalwood water. I believed her. Once, Father caught me cradled in a willow's gentle arms. Another time, I was led like a proud servant into summer's deepest grove. I could name all the fruit.

Winter came. Snow heavy as bone. Our little hut was trapped between help and hell. Father ventured out for pinewood. Mother prayed. Then the howl: the world was bitten by white teeth. We didn't see him until a week had passed. When I approached, he didn't remember who I was. He knelt, cried, called me *god*.

He didn't know that was the day I became a man.

What Remained

They were young
revolutionaries, proud silhouettes
against the wilderness:
one foot out, arms folded, chins lifted
like a dare.
Behind them, a rhododendron—pink,
rising into a looming
peak. Spring
brewed in the clouds, ready to release
something warm.

One happy morning
in the 1980s, they climbed
into a truck and ventured
into the permanent snow.

One died—
he threw himself off a cliff.
One lay bedridden, his lungs
sanded with coal.
Father—lucky man—
took to gambling and alcohol.
Older, he would sit alone by the river
that cascaded south, as if

something might be dredged up,
might reach him like a hand he could hold on to.
Only driftwood came,
carried down in tufts of waves,
swallowed by the fog that seemed
never to lift.

Chess

Father barred the door,
cornered me, a wolf approaching a fawn.
I must have done something terribly wrong,
but I forgot—I bet he had, too—
what had raged a father against his son.
His belt struck like lightning.
Mother, crying, threw herself
against the door, then the window, cursed.
There was pain
even a mother's body couldn't ease.
In despair, she,
clawing at the wooden door,
begged me to apologize,
begged me to promise to be a good boy.
I never did.
I closed my eyes, imagined my bones breaking
into wings.

He would kneel when sober,
sobbed, promised change. I believed him—I always did.
I didn't know forgiveness
was a game of chess. We spent years perfecting it.

Crossing

It was never easy, so you imagined a bridge, hung like a rusted turnpike over the currents that selvaged the ravine with white. You thought of your parents, how every morning they slipped out before you woke, how moonlight frosted their tousled hair.

You sat alone by the fireplace, rehearsing the story they told you—how they loaded pine shafts onto a truck. The road sickness wrung their small bodies. You wanted them home, like you wanted water. They returned at midnight, drenched in sap. You remembered the smell. *Blood of trees*, you used to say, frowning.

If only there had been a bridge to speed them—

They had to push through the miasma of forest, until their bodies wanted to quit and became amorphous, drifting into thin air. That was the end you imagined. They never crossed the river. But you did—followed by twenty years of silence that hovered on the bridge, where your parents had walked every night toward home, toward you.

Oracle

After a reading of turtle shells,
Mother moaned: *He will come at the first crow*
of the rooster. I believed her. What is a child who doesn't
believe their mother? He came on time. That night, cold bit
into my skin. I struggled loose from his grip, looked
behind, thought she would follow. She stood
motionless—a torn trunk blending slowly
into a gathering
of the dark.

Leaving

It was winter, the sky
teal blue. Ice on the dock.
My friends were gone.

I tore one name from my book,
then another. I survived.
I went into spring on horseback.

Behind me, snow heaped
like cream, then scattered.
My coat was the color

of rotten teeth. I was afraid.
The pass was a thing
with gaping mouths.

I wanted to speak—words turned
cold, hardening my tongue.
I was chained to a thought of sleet.

No one was there. The trail
tapered into a bur of cedars:
a warning of what was about to break.

I called it adventure. I called it loss.
I called out to a rhododendron.
What could it know?

Mother—my mother alone—
lantern in hand, knelt
before a god made of stones.

II

Elegy

The gurney creaked. I wheeled her body across the corridor. Her body, wrapped in black, motionless. My steps, a requiem played wrong: each one a faltering tone. At the end, a dim light flashed against the pulse of night. My hands clutched the metal frames

that held her, a shadow barely drawn. Almost touching mine, her fingers tame, tamed. What house of the living could house her death? What house of the dead could take her? Through what gate? I pushed her into dark.

When the Heavenly Dog Swallowed the Sun

The gate to the other world opened. I hid in our thatch hut. There were sounds: hymns, prayers, mumblings. Someone rang a bell. Someone breathed syllables. There was always someone. Mother didn't like visiting relatives—especially the dead ones. Still, she cooked rice topped with a thick piece of pig-head meat, side-dished with complaint. After placing bowls on the table, I was introduced to each of our dead. My body—my young body—became a festival of names.

Full Moon Ghazal

To the moon that hangs old, let's drink,
now everything pales like snow. Drink

to this whitened hour firmly brimming
our cups. Raise it high, this drink

of upturned soil, of loaned water, the best
of this land. Grandfather's drink,

when he halted his plowshare and stared,
the dawn brewing inside the drink.

One day, field-bent, cold, he
wandered elemental, like his drink,

his land, leaving the taste of wheat
and sorghum locked in the drink

to Father, who passed it on to me
the day I was born. A drop of our drink

on my head, unspooling a rill
from the touch: a fleeting chill of a drink

carried by calloused hands—my hands
tremble like earth under blade. Drink

with me, to the moon, to those who waded
into night, to those who follow. Drink!

Pioneer

When he was a young man,
Father's father went
into the heights.

In his dirty backpack, a fold
of chopped paper—his life:
a puddle of ink, skeins of numbers.

The bureau head read them through,
then stashed them in a box
of three hundred documents.

(Three hundred people—
some young, some bent like the trees
on that stunted plateau.)

Father's father asked about the job.
The same man shook his head,
gave him a bus ticket.

He sat in the last row. The road
was long, meandering, like intestines
ripped from an animal.

He closed his eyes. Cold lodged
inside his bones. In his dream:
a dog, a house without a door,

a silence like what was held
in a fist—
he marched on.

Inheritance

They are Tibetan. They are a couple. They wore clothes of harnessed fire that day. They were drowning. Father took them home, offered soup and a shower. They were gone the next morning, leaving behind words like whorls curling into form. There were fireflies where they stayed.

A mute world. A world that exiled my parents to the wild. A hut, like a disemboweled mammal. They came the following winter, robed in glitter. The cold sun battered gold at their steps. They brought meat, barley, and butter. At night they sent a mastiff to guard the yard. They appeared whenever snow carpeted pine treetops.

One day, Father, out hunting, saw their faces painted on a stupa. He took out his khata, wrapped it at the top. He forgot where—only remembered the canyon bending its crooked shoulder.

Mother scolded him. There were things best left undiscovered. She was right. They stopped coming. Daunted, father went on a trip looking for them. In vain. The way was gauzed in fog.

Years later, Father could still hear the mastiff barking, barking in the forest, however dark the night, however far he wandered from home.

The Visit

She traveled a day from the cloud-line, her tiny bound feet supported by a stick. Her face was swarthy as rich soil. On her back, a basket, greased from overuse, strung tight with a thick rope that threatened to break.

We called her *Old Mother*, though in our dialect *mother* sounded like *cat*. She was old. She was a mother. She was a cat. When she arrived, we knew it was summer.

When asked, she lisped—a mix of languages. We picked up words like scalebark, silverfoot, needleblanket, pineapplehorn. It was a place we could never reach—a lost page from a map. She had missing teeth.

I was young back then, I too had missing teeth. I tagged along behind her black dress, a shadow to form. I demanded a gift. She winked. Something sparkled in her eyes, like embers. She didn't stay long.

It was the last day of June in the year 1995. The sky was high, cloudless; waves of blue broke at the ridge. The path led uphill, skirting a giant rock, behind which she disappeared. Where she walked, the scent of a forest surrendered to rain.

The Man from the Mountain

He came to the village at the first sound of thunder. He had fishhook eyes. He hobbled. He stooped. He cursed. His hands twitched. He came only from the south.

I rushed back home, abandoning my tiny playground, his breath at my neck. I shut the door and counted his steps, *duk-duk*, *duk-duk*, until they were swallowed by distance.

Those were long summer days in the forest. My body was a rack of blooming cells. Vexed by mud, the old river roared and tumbled on its narrow bed. He was patrolling the bank.

Through my fingers I could see the small of his back. He was dressed like a moss-eaten rock. No one else could see him.

That day I was taken from the village, I sat alone in the last row of a worn bus. Far off, where my eyes could reach, he reclined against a lush walnut tree. I stared at him, then at the summit behind: a throne.

He waved.

Falling into Earth

I have imagined him
with this creased
landscape woven
into his eyes;
no sky too immense,
no winnowed heaps
of hills too difficult,
no gullied ravines too deep.
Maybe he thinks so too,
one foot on the rusted
rung of the pagoda,
daring the reseda
smoke of spring
to a halt. Steepled
above him and me,
the travertine likeness
of a man (or a buddha
or a fata morgana)
with folding hands,
his imposing shadow
falling into the rock
throat of the earth.
Perhaps we will fall
too, after we ascend

to the heights—there
aspens speak
the language
of the flowing fog.

What Was Carried in the Dark

Like an oak planting a seed,
I planted his face
into the rich hillside of memory.
Soon it was spring. New oaks sprouted.
The village was a cold shade of gray,
patched with rotten planks. I wanted
a cherry tree's pink. Instead,
I had a dry well.
I looked up; the deep blue
shattered like porcelain between clouds.
An eagle soared above mountains that folded
into one another, unconsoled. At the far end
of the path: dust courting dust.
A sunset. Time was an angry mother.
I hid. At midnight, I saw the onyxes
of his eyes. When morning broke,
he was gone. He never came.
He became all there was
to lose—

III

Elegy

Namo Ratna Trayaya. Midnight. The radio spun sutra into air. I was patient, old; I held the radio. The room reeked of incense. If incense was unable to keep her, what use were songs? I used her name as a song. Unable to finish, I cut my tongue with my teeth

as if my teeth could wake my tongue. She was gone, a leaf ferried to the west. I was the ferryman. I opened the casket. She slept. *Prove me wrong*, I said. The casket creaked. I gathered my senses as my senses gathered the last of her. Night salted my eyes.

Death Brought Many Images

This time, his toes,
protruding
from the snow sheet.
I couldn't see his face.
I asked myself: *Did he shave?*
Father covered my eyes,
turned me out to the door.
I sat at the cold end
of the yard, watched adults
threading through the vestibule.
I was left alone; I appreciated that.
I tossed his name on my tongue
until it went numb. It was not
a conjuring—
I was only a boy.
Shame was physical
I began to gasp.
It was a hot summer day.
A hornet was busy hunting
a hive. What did I know
of its appetite, its spite.
I could have caught it;
I let it go—

Darkest Hour

The god of No comes at four, sharp
with the voice of a doctor,
demanding a signature, a blood
fingerprint. The paper
he brings, white
like white, written full
of medical terms;
a verdict:
death.

To us, every statement reeks
of pedantry, every offer
of condolence, disgusting.
The darkest hour is full
of the afternoon heat;
no myth, no
justification.
Just a bed,
a body,
nothing
more.

We'll learn to live on,
much less
than we—

Before He Hanged Himself

He closed the door, bolted it, like any afternoon. A monk came, as if the chant could wake him, as if he would walk, yawning and annoyed, in his greasy slippers to the door.

I sneaked away from his yard, knees bruised, hands dirty. The road, crumbled in dry air, crawled into dark. A parchment cloud unrolled. Wind raced past me, past the silent horizon, lost in a place I never wanted to know.

I Was Told About the Loop Around His Neck

I couldn't believe so, but I remembered
the crooked tree spreading
its canopy like hands in prayer.

Ever since, I avoided the dirt road.

Far off, the bruised shadow
of our village—walls dulled into crust.

Days were filled with the burnt scent of sap.

At night, the snaking roots of grass hissed.

I sat in a wicker chair, imagined myself in water.

Night sky was a frozen lake. Light, unperturbed,
sank like an unmoored mood.

A leaf swayed, as if wanting to speak but knowing better.

I pretended I was an adult. It was easier.

Sometimes before morning, a dog barked, then more joined.

I asked him to come home.

Color of the Moon

High in the grove, she buried him. The upturned earth unpetaled beside her feet. There was the sound of wind combing through trees. The moon was so bright that night, it looked like a blade against the neck. She was alone.

She started to talk to herself every day, until sleep delivered a short promise of peace. Words torn from her chipped teeth became a story no one could understand. Only the wind came, touching her hair like a good husband.

That was how I remembered her that day: body sunk into the chair, head dropped to one shoulder—on her face, almost a smile.

In the Dark

Sometimes it's so dark at night
the world you know disappears.
The willow bloats into shadow.
Suddenly, your east seems west.
No owls hoot—they cannot
tell which way takes you home.

You flail, knowing
your flashlight is of no help.
You point it to the sky, watch
it absorbed like milk into ink.

You need some proof of life. You whistle.
A strange sound comes from the field,
like a scream ripped from a throat.

You close your eyes.
(It makes no difference anyway.)

Sometimes, there's nothing you can do
but stay where you are, hope

the sunrise will lift the darkness, the way
a mortician lifts a coffin's heavy lid.

Sometimes, even death wants a way out.

Drowning of a Shepherdess

Must be the ghost prowling at night,
Grandmother sighed.
She picked up a small stone,
carefully arranged it at the stupa.
Day moon hung low, a dagger
piercing the quilted field.

On the bank, goats roamed free.
The river, confused by swirls and cold,
sputtered mud.
Women began to gather at the water.
Men trudged along,
heads bowed, exchanging gossip.

A slow procession—
like steam blown out of dawn.

Late, much too late,
the sun
had sunk its careless reflection
without a sound.

What the Dead Wanted

We always left food for the dead. But last time, they didn't touch it. No words of gratitude, either. The delivery boy saw the trees gesturing something. He didn't know sign language.

People worried their dead were sick. It was flu season. The village doctor didn't know which herbs to prescribe. In the end, he scribbled something like *tigerpalm roots*—the kind that grow only where no light ever shines—or *just wait for spring.*

I helped Father bring more thatch and blankets to the graveyard. Food, too, with ginger juice to keep our dead warm. Snow filled our boots. We sat at the tombstone. Father lit a cigarette.

Silence was a gray something swallowing our tiny village. We stayed as long as the cigarette lasted. The path home was pocked with rocks.

Suddenly, Grandfather, in his roofed tomb, drew a long sigh. I didn't know better then. I thought it was a falcon diving from the heights.

Tomb Sweeping

Easier to go on foot, where roads docked into grass. Rocks, effaced, re-faced, yielded to sere bracken. No sound, except a gust huckstering dust and gnats to dry hills.

The slope climbed higher, scraping the gut of a copse. Such fear as the sky slushed down. August smoke adhered.

I heaved a sigh—too much of myself among stones.

IV

Elegy

Fire was her flesh. Holding her photo, I knelt before the incinerator. Two of us, again, against the world: one ice, one fire. She lived, or I was dead. No. The collector—Death—came a second time. The collection: bones and ashes on the bitumen floor.

Not her! Not me! I scooped her into an urn. Two scoops. Three. My palms flayed. I was counting—I lost my count. Hell was the red of an urn. A murderer, I fell before the fire of her flesh.

Once Upon a Time

A boy wondered what lay
beyond these intricate peaks,

what paint peeled from a bus
to form its shadow,

what scrap fell from a plane,
what signal plucked like berries in a jungle.

He went out searching.
He thought he could reach the summit.

More rose like waves.
A stupa stood etched in light.

There were secrets kept from children—
like how wolves were guarding

the threshold. Once you stepped
across it, there would be

no way back. The wolves wouldn't let you.
You'd spend your whole life

looking. But the boy didn't know
that yet. He wanted to leave—

he sat by the stupa. Wind brushed
his fingers, a reminder of the tangible

nearness to change. A small lobe
of darkness stuck in his throat.

Looking for Shambhala

I need to believe in my walking. My lungs heave. A choked morning. The land knotted in shade—then a forest of rhododendrons: pink rumpling white. The golden tips of stupas. Prayer flag winds. Beneath me, the river's green recesses. The brambles riot. I'm locked like a fish in two hands. If I could understand every fallen leaf. If I could be naughty as rain. If I could hear whatever a pinecone has to tell—a confession tastes like thistle and I tear my throat open. Alone, I win by losing what I hold dearest: my wound lying far beyond—

Aubade

The field yields at the sound of my boots. I follow myself long before I
know where to go. My head full of this, full of now. The valley,
            smaller than what my eyes can see, festooned in elms, pines, and
banyan trees. Everyone needs a place he doesn't know.

I stop where I shouldn't. The sun, high above, down below. The lake steals.
A falcon glides down, soars up, ignoring me, as I
                                                offer my hot, rapid
breaths to the still, cold air: a token. Then a tree of deer, a rock of bees, a
tomb of feathers. What am I. A compass. The south.

Gold, a little more gold on every branch, and more of me. Silence cuts
silence. Shrills—must be monkeys. Early fall. Deep springs
            converge where they will become ice. But not now. I reach out my
hand. Almost warm, almost afternoon; I hold my face.

Then the haze, as if summer again. Close my eyes. Epiphany. Open my
eyes. Revolution. I'm younger than a chestnut but older
                                                than a mulberry.
I need a handful of seeds to know. A clash of clouds on the mountain
blade. Warped hours of leaves. No way back.

My flesh flowers
in the long hush of seasons—
the valley, old.

Snow Country

dawn:
dark slate
above rabbit tracks.

~

frozen scree;
apparition
of a trail; kombu hills.

~

trees stripped
to gray; a sprawling road;
no one came—

~

no one left.

The Pavilion of Flying Clouds

Mountains gallop away, further,
lost,
a lavender morning.
The vast flow of this world—the sky
rests on top.

Countless trees crawl upward,
downward,
becoming one,
like smoke breathed through
moss-colored cracks in cliffs.

My boots
above paired purslanes—
no road for me.

My mouth opens,
a hymn
folds into forgotten earth.

Drought

That summer, air raised
grit to our nostrils; fire
burned in the sirocco,
driving men into the shallow
shade of trees.
We could smell what was coming:
fruit violated by heat,
weeklong sewage,
our bodies disdained
by salt and dandruff.
In the valley, the river ran
like a stitch on exsiccated skin.
Rocks sprouted
out of the pond, becoming hot iron,
becoming that July
when the textured wind
weighed us down, stuffed
our lungs with cotton.

The elder declared no rain
for the season and stood
a tablet beneath a spruce,
a collation of rice cakes placed
in front. A plea.

Simple times back then.
We got what we asked for.
When the first drop fell
on the chapped field,
he sat alone, smoked—
the color of grain
rising from his pipe.

Ode

When I was small, the world was smaller,
hidden in your lush groves. I did not

need to outgrow your burned afternoons,
or frosty mornings before the red of day

tinted your rocky girth, coaxing roosters
to the roof, people to the field.

Your shadow, thrown onto hills
vaulted into a higher sky,

until rain brought it down to earth, to the eyes
of farmers who feared for the harvest.

You held the fallen in your palms,
returned it to the high.

There were always brave people,
who drove in during raging seasons.

Trucks full of goods you could not
provide: batteries, gas, secondhand

televisions, letters from a city.
At your foot, they stopped, rested

the night. It was good to end
a day like this—stars that nested

on your shoulder would watch in silence,
then burn out, among a few lamps of home.

Gold

I watched him walk into the torrent.
The water that lapped his waist
blew apart like silk. His basket
pulled him down, balanced
by the wooden hoe he held.
He bent over, still,
an old heron. The blade cleaved
the surface that closed fast,
striving to hide a secret.
Then the sound of rocks
drifted up, swallowed by waves
that tore at his thin body. Every twist
of his muscle, joy; every hour,
hallowed. The sun lodged
among pebbles like gold.

We marched home past rows
of vines and hawthorns,
proud soldiers. We laughed.
Our laughter sailed
across twenty years and lands now,
scattered among reeds where I sit,

listening. The river runs,
bypassing hills that hulk
into my father's golden ravine.

Chasing the Sun

I

People wake long before roosters.
There's much to do:
herding cattle, watering corn, scything down
weeds good for pigs.

Then they see the sun.

They've lived long enough in the mountains to know
the brief window of joy—the warmth
seeps into their skin; their cells bloom
like poppies.

They put down the work. Someone even yells.
More come out of their houses, flock
to the rugged ledge.

The world is half light, half the color of coal.

II

The sun is a shepherd.

For a moment, it seems possible to forget
the brutality of this place.
It's easier to be happy with life
when there's something to walk toward.

They understand the myth of Kuafu.
He died of insatiable thirst.
His staff became a peach forest.

Sometimes I wonder if it's the best way to die—
having an unfulfilled yearning,
like how ephemerae are remembered
for wanting, but never getting
another day.

I've charted many courses for them in my memory,
pretended they all have
happy endings.

Of course I wish them well, these people; I do

let them go, each to their own story—I walk
into the space they leave behind.

In the Dream I Survived

Half the village burned down. We walked to the far end of the grove. Mother brought all her candles.

—

Ash in the wind. Ash the color of fish struggling for air. I covered my mouth with walnut leaves. In the shrubs, crickets squealed.

—

The dead floated down the creek. They were hardly dressed. It would rain. That was the hope. They sucked in black air, spoke algae.

—

It was June. The power station devoured muddied currents and coughed fire. Power lines cut a sullen dusk.

—

Alerted by soot on our heads, the cows looked sideways. One approached carefully, nuzzled my hand.

—

A scarecrow hung from a barn beam, half its body singed, almost gone. Its eye sockets stuffed with charcoal.

—

We huddled around a campfire. Not enough, I made a hat out of weeping willows.

—

The elder was meant to appease the fire god with a pig's head, three cups of baijiu, and long red teakwood incense.

—

Flies came. Then frogs. Then a pack of wolves.

Crows hovered. *Cover your eyes too,* Father warned me. He dug his fingers into the earth and scooped a stone.

—

The road un-ribboned, ascended into thick clouds. The gate to the high heaven was swaddled in smoke.

V

Elegy

Her urn against my chest, I walked among trees. The road to the grave was long. She had a long life. I should be happy and bring a smile to my weary face. *Smile*, I told myself. Her house now the lasting green. How would she receive my visit?

How would my visit free her from the earth? *Do visit*—she said. Or was it from my mouth? Must be the wind. She must have spoken in wind. Shrubs stirred. I hid behind skin. Her urn, my chest, our futile lives.

I Wake to a World That Has Rejected Me Many Times

In the dream, I am
        a child. The river upturns

white to my palms.
        Reflection of

a lotus plucked from a dry stem;
        then silence, like

between prayers.
        Cold boulders thrust

images in water, hardened
        when evening erupts

from the gorge.
        I scoop a handful of hues

turning flesh, turning hollow.
        I try to save the light stained

with things, to bring a saint out
        of a monster. In another dream

I am the monster baring teeth,
mouth open to shredded

breaths. Hurt is the mantra
I swallow.

Another Summer, Fujiang

I follow a ghost down the stream.
Tiers of waves come unclustered, lost
at the bank. Sounds soar, as if in speech.

The banister crawls—wet and black—
into a gullet. Too many people.
I'm alone. Summer trapped in air.

Years later feels like years ago, though
for the first time I enjoy this stroll, a word
stumbling into a sentence, finding itself

just right. The difference is, I'm much older;
truth is, I'm still a hurt child. The same
street, like an accent passed down

through generations, still rich with intonation.
At every bend, squalid buildings lounge
into tireless traffic. At night,

the lonesomeness of yellow lights.
Peddlers sell chili on bikes, the scent furrowing
deep into the white smoke of barbecue stands.

They smile—I don't know how
to respond to their *Hahhhloh* anymore.
Any kindness would break me.

But my arrival
suggests my imminent departure. My heart
wants a place I might never find

worthier. I continue my walk, knowing
I've lit a candle for the time past,
and for the time to come.

Landscape for the Lost

The plateau holds this town:
clouds are calluses. No rain,
air heaps dust in my eyes.
End of summer. I don't know how
to respond to the sudden change.
Sweat tongues my skin, an animal.
A far sunset; bony Lu Mountain;
colorful buildings rise
from groves of wilting trees.
I'd like to trace every footprint
of the child I was, to greet
every stranger: each syllable
carries the tones of two languages,
as my body carries yesterday and now,
whenever I flee the long arm
of memory.
                        Here I am,
cowering at a brick wall.
Darkness, conjured from each crack,
forms a shape on my body—
I can almost lose myself. I toss
my cigarette to the breeze, admire
the spark's fatalistic curve.
Almost evening, I have nowhere to go.

Homebound

You know it's there, held
where the heat blasts into sand.

Landslides and gravel will slow
your car before it climbs

onto the fissured road
like an ant on split bark.

You let the power lines guide you
southward, chasing the glint

as it chips away at the immense
sprawl of scrub, until they

yield to an impression, a thin memory.
You'd lose your way, if not

for a swinging signpost. Its paint
haunts like déjà vu. A swarm of dust

greets you like motherless
children tugging at your shirt.

You stand alone.
The familiar silence reigns

as it did twenty years ago,
a pregnant question.

Nobody knows what became
of the people you left behind.

Muli

Spanned by the Shambhala sky, the dark ridges
heaved. Streets ascended into moonlight.

Flying eaves, blessed by strings of prayer flags,
held rings of lotus, or fire, or clouds, or verses

of Heart Sutra flowing like air. In the town square
a stupa, white-bloused, gold-crowned, entouraged

by bronze mani wheels, imparted blessings
in a language I longed to understand. Between lanes

muralled doors were warm to the touch,
even when winter threatened cuts on my skin.

In the breeze: the scent of butter tea and roasted potatoes.
A woman led a horse satcheled with corn. And me?

I had trouble sleeping. The room I bunked in
with three travelers smelled of fern. They slept, heads

on greasy bags. I wondered what they saw in me,
who clutched a heart like a hidden book.

I was almost eighteen. I'd been promised a future;
I made my way to the past. In the holy town,

I sought a ghost—robed in a monastery's pine smoke—
to tell me a story, in which I could be found.

Like an Enemy, Like Love

I dreamed of it, as if it were there,
soaked in the bleeding sun.
A few shacks—
holes on every plate, like cataract eyes
gazing into the shadow that fled
from light. The past
was something I unearthed each day:
every shadow returned.
But no people would appear,
no ghosts conjured from engravings.
I stood at the gate, knowing
one step forward would be one step back
into the heaviness of loss.
How tiny this village:
pulped saffrons, empty silos, a fallen stupa,
sparrows hopping to no end,
to no ears the mill spinning a hymn.
Only mountains remained, cold and stony,
bony hands long forgetting how to pray.
I fell to my knees—

End of the World

I remember the village without a name.
I remember the light as the last note of an echo.
Timeless gray, broken tiles;
weed-riot, bony birds;
a group of foresters owning no trees;
a ranch where goats run amok;
a story told by many, but heeded by no ears.
To reach it, I drive into the heights
but never turn right.
Dogs come bringing morning
with frost biting their hair;
at night, moonlight stacks
like boulders on bald mountains.

~

A lamp burns like a saint
carrying death on his back.

I knock.

A boy whispers, *they are still*
two horse-rides away.
You don't need to

hurry.

~

There's rain
to beat the azure sky into earth.
The sound of shattered air barrels
against the roof, sullen
like a woman pounding her thigh.

If this is how the sky rises
from the mud—

Mother knew it;
she swept silt off the door.

~

The river.

I cup my hands and press its jade
surface to my lips. I let it drink me,
until memories of my ancestors
are drained into its body.

Father gave me pebbles soaked with years
of warmth from the highland;
he gave me fish I could not name;
he gave me waterlogged driftwood;
he gave me grievance.

Now waves break at my feet,
drowning a voice I once knew.

~

Morning fog. I drew
a winding path on the windowpane:
there was a kite; there was grass;
there was a boy.

I was alone then;
I wanted toy guns, Barbies, mini-dinosaurs.

One day, I buried them
at the root of a swaybacked tree.

~

Once I climbed high
and imagined wings.
The valley was deep.
The slope shimmered in summer.
Houses scattered
like lanterns forgotten along a forest trail.

I became smaller;
I wanted to soar where the day stored its promised pink.

A world beyond this world.

I looked up to a sky known and foreign—

~

One by one, houses fell
into silence; one by one, they fell.
Saffron mornings.

Now, the saffrons are blooming.
Now, a whirlwind of hoofs.

There on the slope, a pile of stones.

In the Hospital Mother Apologizes

New Year's Eve.
The countdown falls.
Mother,
bones broken
where her hand
swallows wrist.
I'm again hiding
in the comfort
of distance. My day,
her night—two sides
of a coin.
On the phone screen:
her face; the cold
blue of the ceiling;
light warped
in refraction.
She waves
her good hand.
I tell a lie: I will
be alright.
A brief silence
stalls in my throat.
Pain is a real thing
so I cut it open:

a bleeding
of words.
My trembling voice—
a bluet by her head.

Epilogue

I left 915. That day, I became water, or time, or a falling leaf—anything that could not find its way back to where it began.

I sat in the bus. I looked back. The mountains loomed, broken, abandoned to their immense expanse, too vast to hold a shape. The Litang River, swollen with silt, carved through the ravine, lost to a place I'd only heard of. The village—my village—a scab on the writhing body of the land, vanished as the bus pulled away panting like an old beast. It was a summer day. Yet snow still gleamed on the peaks—perpetual, untouched.

Eight years passed. Eight short, long years. When I returned, I sat beneath my parents' low eaves and tried to recognize the faces I had once sewn into names—names buried in my memory like a song I always knew I'd forget. I had forgotten I was no longer that child.

I turned my eyes to the familiar summits. Even they seemed taller—no, impossibly tall. Or had I become so unbearably small that even memory might forget me? In a photo, I saw myself—four years old, reclining against a pink rhododendron. The child was a ghost. I couldn't—couldn't look him in the eyes.

No one knew I was a murderer. The day I left the village, I killed myself. I murdered my parents. I slaughtered everyone dear to me. This life—this poetry, this distance—is a mausoleum I built with my own hands.

A man approached. Perhaps he knew me. He was certainly old enough. Perhaps my face reminded him of someone—someone long lost in time. Should I speak? Should I say, "Yes, it's me"? Touch my face—touch it, and you will know my name.

Now say my name—

You who knew me as the boy once called Ocean. Not the word. The weight. The salt and wave of it.

Say my name, Mother, the way you used to sing your prayers—soft, beautiful, futile. Say it for all the pain you carried, and all the pain still waiting for you.

Say my name, Father, the way you spoke about your stolen dreams. Say it like the wind chasing what it has already lost.

Say my name, Grandpa, like the snow sweeping past your door. You closed it and walked into the mist. I was too young to follow.

Say my name, Grandma, in your endless stories of the town you longed to return to. You raised us all, then were gone without a sound. You didn't die alone.

Say my name, godparents of Father—devout Tibetans—say it like your morning sutra. You took my parents under your wings. They survived. I didn't know where you were buried.

Say my name, man from the south, in your mumblings. I feared you. I apologize. Your madness wasn't a reason to be cast away.

Say my name, aunt in black, in your Yi language I wish I could understand. Every summer you came, mushrooms and laughter tucked in your basket.

Say my name, Zhang, the way you might have before you hanged yourself. Your beer bottle still held your breath, a message to reach no one.

Say my name, little shepherdess, like you once called your goats. Your voice was a song strung through the field. I still see you in rivers.

Say my name, bus driver, like you did during that the long, tedious drive. A landslide took you, and the bus. A ferryman swallowed by the tide.

Say my name, villagers, all of you. Say it the way you used to: *Yang*. No one else ever called me that. Only you knew what I was meant to be—an idea of the infinite blue: the sea drawing me in, vast and unyielding, but never free.

Now, I speak my name. I'm a poet, my verse my scalpel. I cut myself open to give birth to the dead. They look at me with marble eyes. They want to speak. Their language lives in my voice.

What do I have to offer? I was a child. I want to remain a child. I am the tension on the bow that draws the arrow. To lose myself—that is my destiny.

Notes

This book's opening epigraph is taken from L.P. Hartley's luminous novel *The Go-Between.*

"Elegy, in Five Parts" began as a nonce form I created during Carl Phillips's prosody class.

"Elegy" incorporates a line, *Namo Ratna Trayaya*—"homage to the three jewels"—from the Great Compassion Mantra of Avalokiteśvara, traditionally sung at funerals.

"Elegy"and "Darkest Hour" are dedicated to XianXing Wen, my dearest Grandma.

"The Shrine" is written after Eleanor Goodman.

"Crossing" is written after Esteban Rodríguez.

"Leaving" is an ekphrastic response to *Power of the Caves*, a symbolist tempera painting by Nicolas Roerich, 1925.

"What Was Carried in the Dark" borrows a line from Ocean Vuong.

"Once Upon a Time" is written after Maggie Smith, with a line borrowed from her.

"Looking for Shambhala" refers to 香巴拉, a spiritual kingdom in Tibetan Buddhist tradition. Muli Tibetan Autonomous County is referred to—by some—as the last Shambhala.

"Drought" is written after Ron Rash.

"Ode to a Mountain" is dedicated to Sunzi Shan, or Bamboo Shoot Mountain, whose name you won't find on any map.

"Chasing the Sun" incorporates an ancient Chinese myth about Kuafu, who chased the sun across the sky until he perished of thirst.

"In the Dream I Survived" borrows a line from Charles Simic.

"I Wake to a World That Has Rejected Me Many Times" is written after Sarah Ghazal Ali.

"Another Summer, Fujiang" is dedicated to the city of Shehong.

Acknowledgments

My deepest gratitude to the many amazing people who have walked into my life, seen me, and believed in me as a poet. Thank you for making this book possible.

To David Tait, one of the very first to see a poet in me. Thank you for all the encouragement. Thank you for being the first reader of many of my poems.

To Felicity Plunkett, my first teacher of poetry writing. Thank you for guiding me on the road to finding my voice. Thank you for your trust and encouragement.

To Mary Jo Bang, for the mentorship in and out of the classroom. Thank you for teaching me the art of poetic precision and lyrical indirection. Thank you for offering feedback on many of the poems in the book.

To Carl Phillips, thank you for the teaching and the conversations about poetic mystery and clarity, which opened new dimensions in my understanding of poetry.

To Niki Herd, thank you for the teaching and for introducing me to the wonderful art of prose poetry.

To Eduardo C. Corral, thank you for our conversations about the lyrical, which has helped shape many of these poems, especially in revision.

To Katherine Finneran, thank you for teaching me the art of memoir writing.

To Ilya Kaminsky, thank you for seeing something worthy in this book. *Dancing in Odessa* was one of the first poetry books that made me want to be a poet. I want to live in your words. Thank you for your tireless work to bring peace and justice to Ukraine.

To Sneha Subramanian Kanta, thank you so much for all your trust, support and encouragement ever since I began writing and publishing.

To Sarah Song Xiaran, my deepest gratitude for gifting me such a wonderful cover image. I couldn't have asked for a better one.

To Varuna, The Australian National Writers' House. To my masterclass alumni, thank you for helping me to grow in ways I could never have imagined.

To the MFA program at Washington University in St. Louis, thank you for such precious time to write and learn. To my brilliant cohort, who read many of these poems and offered invaluable feedback. Tola Sylvan, Marc-Anthony Valle, Ameen Animashaun, Jeron Hicks. I couldn't ask for a better cohort. It has been an honor for me to share this journey with you.

To the kind poets of Shanghai Poetry Workshop, now Inkwell Poetry Workshop. Thank you for being there and helping me grow when I first started to write poetry.

To Martha Rhodes, Ryan Murphy, Rowan Sharp, and all the kind editors of Four Way Books, thank you for trusting this book and bringing it into the world. It's a dream come true.

I'd like to also thank the following people for their support—either directly or indirectly: Tiffany Troy, Tammy Lai-Ming Ho, Jane Huffman, Patrick Schiefen, Johan Uusitalo, Monica Tao, Ran Xu, Eva Wang, Erno Chen, Lei Wang, Nicole Callräm, Esteban Rodríguez, Andrew Yang Lin, Qi Sun, Apollo Chastain, David Ehmcke, Syd Wesley, Ariana Benson, Temperance Aghamohammadi, Zain Baweja, Mikaela Hoover, Edwardson Ukata, Amelia Schofalvi, Lydia Golitz, Cameron Maynard, Arun Dhillon, Bob Henkel, Lavinia Xu, Winniebell Xinyu Zong, Cass Garison, and many more.

I'm grateful to the editors of the following journals and anthologies in which poems have appeared, often in various forms: *Action, Spectacle*; *Allium*; *The Arkansas International*; *Australian Poetry Journal*; *Cider Press Review*; *FOLIO Literary Journal*; *Harvard Review*; *The Indianapolis Review*; *The Kenyon Review*; *Meridian*; *The Orison Anthology* (*Best Spiritual Literature*); *Parentheses Journal*; *A Personal History of Home: An Anthology*; *Schuylkill Valley Journal*; *The Shanghai Literary Review*; *Tupelo Quarterly*; *Twyckenham Notes*; 声韵诗刊 (*Voice and Verse Poetry Magazine*); and *The Westchester Review*.

And as always, my everlasting love to my family.

To my cat, Susu, for being the eternal sunshine in my life.

To my husband, Steven, for unwavering love.

About the Author

Aiden Heung (he/they) is a Chinese poet born in a Tibetan Autonomous town. After working as a traveling salesman for years, he recently relocated to St. Louis, USA. His poems have been published in *Australian Poetry Journal*, *Harvard Review*, *The Kenyon Review*, *The Yale Review*, 声韵诗刊 (*Voice and Verse Poetry Magazine*), and many other places. He is a finalist for the DISQUIET Prize, a winner of the International Proverse Poetry Prize, and the recipient of 2025 Elinor Benedict Poetry Prize, selected by Diane Seuss. He and his work have been generously supported by Varuna, The National Writers' House (Australia) and Swatch Art Peace Hotel residency (Switzerland/ Shanghai, China). He holds an MFA in creative writing from Washington University.

Four Way Books is grateful to those individuals who participated in our Build a Book Program. They are:

Anonymous (10), Robert Abrams, Debra Allbery, Maggie Anderson, Kathy Aponick, Sally Ball, Jean Ball, Victor Basta, Adria Bernardi, Richard Blanchard, Laurel Blossom, adam b. bohannon, Lee Briccetti, Anthony Cappo, Anne Babson Carter, Cyrus Cassells, Jennifer Christman, Peter Coyote, Kwame Dawes, Michael Anna de Armas, Brian Komei Dempster, Patrick Donnelly, Lynn Emanuel, Joan Frank, Rigoberto González, Rachel Eliza Griffiths, Catherine Grossman, Naomi Guttman and Jonathan Mead, Beth Harrison, Jeffrey Harrison, KT Herr, Carlie Hoffman, Melissa Hotchkiss, Thomas and Autumn Howard, Parker Howe Foundation, Catherine Hoyser, Linda Susan Jackson, Elizabeth Jackson, Liz Janik, Marilyn Johnson, Deborah and Maria Jonas-Walsh, Elizabeth J. Kandall, Maeve Kinkead, Lindsay and John Landes, David Lee and Jamila Trindle, Rodney Terich Leonard, Howard Levy, Owen Lewis and Susan Ennis, Ralph and Mary Ann Lowen, Maja Lukic, Ricardo Alberto Maldonado, Donna Masini, Cleopatra Mathis, Lupe Mendez, Dale Neal, Mary Jane Nealon, Kathy Nelson, Marilyn Nelson, Nicole Nevadunsky, Kimberly Nunes, Rebecca and Daniel Okrent, Cathy McArthur Palermo, Marcia Pelletiere, Megan Pinto, Martha Rhodes, Paula Rhodes, Laurie Rosenblatt, Lyris Schonholz, Soraya Shalforoosh, Jennifer Skeele, Mary Slechta, Page Hill Starzinger, Sarah Stone, Yerra Sugarman, Marjorie and Lew Tesser, Reed Turchi, Maria Walsh, Martha Webster and Robert Fuentes, Calvin Wei, George Whalen Jr., Mark Wunderlich, Kathleen Zimmerman, and Carol Zoref.